SEVEN DAYS IN

FLORENCE

JOHN SHANLE

SEVEN DAYS IN

FLORENCE

JOHN SHANLE

A PARABLE OF TIMELESS SPIRITUAL LESSONS

Library of Congress Catalog Card Number: 99-095142

ISBN 0-9674459-0-6

WITH ALL MY LOVE TO MEREDITH

MANY THANK YOUS TO THE FOLLOWING:

To Grandpa for allowing me to see Italy...
To Donna and Don at Construct for the all-important design
To Meg Laurie for answering 1,000 questions
To Chris Roerdon for dotting the i's and crossing the t's
To Leslie at Wordwise for yet another draft
To David C. for his virgin reading and Forza La Juve Gol!!!

"Expect all of your tomorrows

to resemble all of your yesterdays

unless you change today."

SEVEN DAYS IN

FLORENCE

JOHN SHANLE

A PARABLE OF TIMELESS SPIRITUAL LESSONS

CHAPTER **ONE**

It was nine P.M. when the bell over the door sounded, alarming Signore Vernola that one last customer had entered his bookstore. The customer strolled in as Vernola was preparing to turn the sign over on his window, letting the world, or at least the city of Florence, know that he was closed for the night. Although Italian by birth and a life-long citizen of Florence, he specialized in English books, catering to the high number of American students in Florence.

As Vernola eyed the anxious young man who was fingering through the books, he was hoping that the gentleman's buying intentions were quick and simple, probably a USA Today, or anything in English that would alleviate a bout of homesickness. Sometimes all it took was a baseball score from home to put someone at ease, even though thousands of miles away from home. A home that was more of an idea than a place.

The gray-haired store owner realized that closing time was becoming later by the second, as the probable student was walking up and down every aisle in the store, apparently intent on finding something. His search was now five minutes old.

Michael was a twenty-year-old American student who had been in Florence for six long months and would be on his way home in a couple of weeks. For the first four months of his visit, he did nothing but count the days until he could again board the plane headed home, home to the safe and familiar. A senior, he had one semester left until he walked across the stage to receive his diploma and the venture out into the real world.

For some reason, though, he was no longer excited to go home, no longer captivated to head back to his comfort zone. He had some anxiety and uneasiness about returning and he decided to find a book to answer some of the questions swirling through his head.

It was nine-fifteen when Michael decided to abandon his futile search and ask the store owner for help. Michael had been in the shop a couple of times before, although during those times his purchases revolved around academic material only, nothing personal, such as now.

"Parla Inglese?" asked Michael.

"Yes, yes, I speak English," replied the old man. "Can I help you find something?"

"Yes, you can, sir. In what aisle do you keep the self-help books?"

"Self-help books? You mean those Cliff Notes on living? Well we, or at least I, don't carry those. I understand that they are quite popular where you are from, though. Michael, may I ask why you are interested in such a book?"

"How did you know my name was Michael?" he asked.

"Just a guess. It's a popular American name, no? Back to my question, if you don't mind. Why do you need such a book? Why do you need an instruction guide to your life? Isn't it up to you to plot the moves you must make, the goals you must set, and so on?"

The discussion was getting much more personal than Michael had anticipated. All he wanted was a yes or no answer from the man. Michael didn't know why, but he intended to continue to hold up his end of the discussion.

"I'll tell you why. I'm going home in two weeks, graduating in a few months, and I have no clue as to what I should do with my life. I have no desire to sit behind some desk until I'm sixty. I'd rather have time than money. Still, I guess I'm looking for answers, answers that elude Mom and Dad, or that the Bible's parables cannot explain."

The clock struck nine-thirty as the two men from completely different worlds chatted on. Signore Vernola didn't mind, though. He did more than just sell books. The elder gentleman was also in the business of helping people, and Michael, in his eyes, seemed worthy of such help.

CHAPTER TWO

"Tell you what Michael. Let's close up and take our discussion elsewhere. I don't want people to think I have longer hours all of a sudden," joked Vernola. "By the way, I'm Signore Vernola."

They found a table at an outdoor café that overlooked the Piazza Signoria, which was, as usual, teeming with tourists. The surroundings were vintage Italy. The locals, on mopeds, were dodging lazy tourists whose attention was focused on the gelato they were eating. Bells rang, pigeons scattered in countless directions and late night soccer matches on television boomed from the bars. Groans outnumbered cheers as the beloved team from Florence was losing to the giants of Italy, Juventus.

"Michael, you are not the first student to wander into my shop with more on his mind than simply books. There must be something about the Italian way of life that provokes questions on your part. Please, hear me out.

"Michael, I'd like to help you if you don't mind. Although I was unable to sell you the book you were looking for, I can offer you something even greater and much more valuable. Would you care for me to continue?

The young American nodded eagerly as a glass of water was glued to his lips.

"My guess is that upon graduation you are scheduled to star in a play whose script was written by everyone except you. Your interest is low and you are looking for guidance.

"Michael, if you can give me three things, just three simple things, I can personally guarantee that you never set foot into a bookstore again, at least not down the self-help aisle. Give me three small things and you'll forever be able to help yourself, so to speak.

"You will need a pen, a notebook, and... seven days in Florence."

Michael agreed quickly, not giving it much thought, as he placed his glass down on the table. He had a plane ticket that kept him in Italy at least ten more days and a notebook and pen occupying his wooden nightstand back in his apartment. He though the whole situation seemed a bit surreal. The man knew his name, even though Vernola credited it to luck, and their meeting seemed almost preordained. Roll the dice, roll the dice, Michael, said part of himself, and with that, he smiled at his elder in confirmation.

"Okay, you're on, sir. Seven days in Florence and I'll be the author of my own book and life. It's a deal!"

Signore Vernola smiled, although he knew what the young man's response would be all along.

The two shunned the waiter's request for any further service, except Vernola asked for a clean napkin and the waiter's pen. The activity continued on in the ancient square and Vernola spread the napkin out on the tablecloth and commenced his writing.

The napkin read as follows:

Monday-The Doctor

Tuesday-The Priest

Wednesday-The Curator

Thursday-The Farmer

Friday-The Teacher

Saturday-The Grave Digger

Sunday-

Signore Vernola stopped writing, clicked the pen, and handed the napkin over to Michael, who stared at it, and as he began to wonder about the napkin's content, the store owner began his explanation.

"Michael, this is your itinerary for the week. Starting tomorrow, each day you shall visit these gentleman and each day they will provide you with

a new lesson, idea, something to take back home with you. Something that will be with you forever, I hope. Each teacher will be giving you an idea to enter into your notebook."

Vernola took the napkin back momentarily, just long enough to jot an address down next to each day. But still, no actual names, just titles.

"They will all be awaiting your visit Michael. Just show up and the rest will take care of itself.

"I know you are probably wondering why Sunday is blank, without an appointment. Sunday is the most important day because on that day you will learn the most important lesson of all."

Vernola added one final suggestion to the student. "Please come and say goodbye to me next Sunday. I should be in the store, just try not to cut it so close to nine o'clock, okay?

"Yet I have one rule! Come only if you are able to fill in the blank next to Sunday in your notebook. For if Sunday's lesson eludes you, the other six won't be able to help you at all. Good luck, Michael. Keep the faith and you'll be all right."

The two exchanged handshakes and good-byes. Michael watched the old man disappear into the night. He glanced down at the napkin, still a bit hazy about what was unfolding. He had the eerie sensation that he wasn't the first "student" to embark on this weeklong journey. He wasn't the first to leave Signore Vernola's bookstore with more than just a book. He carefully placed the napkin into his jacket and headed home.

As Michael climbed the stairs up to his apartment, Sunday's lesson played on his mind. Feelings of fear and excitement collided as Michael opened the door. Tomorrow, his true education was to commence.

CHAPTER THREE

Monday's appointment wasn't until nine A.M., so Michael headed to the market early. After buying his daily pasta and bread, he decided to wander through the two-story indoor market, since he still had some time to kill before lesson number one.

He marveled at the Italian diet and how everyone ate whatever they wanted, whenever they wanted. Everyone stayed thin because they walked all day out of necessity, not from guilt-induced exercise. The second floor of the market was as loud as usual, women of the city filling their baskets with that day's fresh produce. People here shopped daily instead of throwing two weeks' worth of frozen food into a cart. Everyone paid in cash. You didn't stand in a line a mile long while someone wrote a check for two dollars worth of food. Florentines lived one day at a time, finding pleasure in tasks that Michael hadn't previously paid any attention to.

The food vendors in the market resembled characters he thought of as found in Hollywood: actors, comedians and singers, all selling fruits and vegetables. They sang while speaking with their hands, and greeted everyone on a first name basis. There were girls selling strawberries who looked as if they could be runway models, men juggling apples, and vendors who didn't speak English, which meant Michael had to brush up on his language skills if he were to do business with them. By attending an American school and reading the Herald-Tribune every day, Michael hadn't exactly accelerated the learning process.

Michael's watch said eight forty-five, and he decided to head over to see his first teacher, the Doctor. That was it, no name. Simply, the Doctor.

Michael caught a bus that took him within a block of 18 Via Faenza. The American found the office and headed up the narrow stairs.

Who do I ask to see, Michael thought to himself. The thought lasted about ten steps until he opened the office door. A smiling receptionist offered Michael a chair and disappeared. Michael shunned the Italian magazines in front of him and waited. Keep the faith, he thought to himself.

Minutes later, a tall man, forty-ish, appeared and extended his hand out to Michael. "Thank you for coming, Michael," said the Doctor. Another person who knows my name, thought the American.

"Mr. Vernola spoke to me last night. He informed me that I had the privilege of being your first lesson. I see that you are equipped with pen and paper, so please follow me."

The two headed back to an office that had framed degrees galore hanging on the walls. Lesson One was underway.

"Michael you are welcome to copy down every word that I say into your notebook. However, I find that it's more effective if you simply listen, listen and write only these three words…"

Monday-Find Your Treasure

"Find your treasure, Michael. Find you treasure. That is the most important point of my entire speech." Michael dropped his pen on his notebook, crossed one leg over his other knee, and began to listen.

"Michael, haven't you ever wondered why people let me play God? It's because they don't think God can do a good enough job. I deal with people and illness all day long. Most of the pain is caused by unhappiness and self-doubt. When you live with that day in, day out, it's no wonder that hospitals are the biggest businesses in the world. I find it odd that all my patients dismiss cancer, heart attacks, and whatever else you'd like to fill in as normal parts of life. They're not. This brings us to your treasure.

"Most people, Michael, are walking around on empty. An emptiness that can be alleviated momentarily with a new car or vacation, yet never cured. The reason behind this is that most people haven't found their treasure, and those who have are afraid to follow where it might lead. Please stick with me, Michael, as I bring God, The Light, or whatever you choose to call Him, into the equation. But He factors heavily into my discussion, as well as those that you'll hear throughout the rest of the week.

"Before each of us leaves Heaven to come and visit Earth for a while, God puts a treasure into our hearts. A gift, a talent, something that will bring us great joy and happiness if it is discovered and put to use. Some people look for it in church, others in the mountains, the rest might try to find it in a book. Those who refuse to acknowledge its existence usually come and see me quite often, thinking I might have it. Your treasure can be found in only one spot. It's inside your heart, and only you have access to it. Some think it is a difficult thing to find, but fear not, Michael, go someplace where you shall be alone and focus on your heart. It will reveal the answers that you need.

"Your treasure is the thing that gives you goosebumps when you're doing it. The thing that you would do if it were impossible to fail. The thing that your heart says yes to, even when your mind says no. For me, Michael, it was becoming a doctor and helping people. If I had only two weeks in which to live, I'd practice medicine until my last breath. It's what I love to do.

"Let me warn you though, young man. If you choose not to obey your heart, your days will be long and hard. You may chase material goals for a while, but it will nag at you through your days. You'll try to chase the voice away with work, alcohol, sex or media. But it will never go away, so listen to its message about what you can contribute to the world. And when you find it, have the courage to follow it, regardless of where it may take you. God bless you, Michael. I wish you the best of luck."

With those words, the doctor shook Michael's hand, not expecting any questions. Michael stood and stared down at the three words on his paper and hoped that he would take them with him back home. He didn't know what his treasure was, but he was certain his heart held the answer. He was confident he would find his treasure. He had to.

Michael's bus ride home allowed his mental chatter to surface. He was surprised that the Doctor who had given him his first lesson was American. He looked at those on the bus and wondered who among them had found their treasure. Were they working at jobs they hated? Were they going to wait until they were sixty-five to find their passion?

And what about Sunday's lesson? Would he be able to fill in the blank that Signore Vernola required?

CHAPTER FOUR

Tuesday morning's sunshine reflected Michael's enthusiasm as he woke up eager to tackle his next lesson. He woke early with the sun and went for a run along the Arno River. He enjoyed being outside with the morning silence as his only companion. The street lights went off as he made his way down Via Nazionale and headed home to get ready for his next lesson. A quick bowl of cereal, then a peek at the newspaper and he was off. Signore Vernola's bookstore was along the way to his next lesson, but he knew that he must wait until Sunday night, provided he had done the work that Vernola required.

Tuesday's lesson with the Priest was to be held at the Duomo, the jewel synonymous with Florence the world over. To the locals, the cathedral was a sign of the city's wealth and power, unrivaled in Italy at the time of its creation in the fifteenth century. Michael thought it made for a skyline unrivaled in the world. It was Florence.

Michael walked with his notebook toward the cathedral and made it by nine o'clock. Pigeons scattered in his path as he dodged a few camera-laden tourists and made his way inside. He had no clue as to what the Priest looked like, or his name, or anything. But he silenced his mental chatter and stared up at the ceiling that could have covered a football field. As he was ogling its height and admiring the courage of those who had built it, a short, stocky gentleman approached him.

"Good morning, Michael. Thank you for being on time. Are you ready to get started?"

Another American, Michael thought to himself. Did someone fly these guys in just for him?

Michael followed the Priest up a spiral staircase that took them to a small balcony overlooking the church floor. It provided them with a bird's-eye view of those in prayer. The Priest was silent as he looked down at those on their knees who were in conference with God.

"Michael, my son, open your book to Tuesday and write down the following…"

Tuesday- Fear is Man's creation.
Faith is God's gift to Man.
Faith is much stronger than Fear.

Michael wrote hurriedly, not expecting the Priest to repeat himself.

"Finished," the Priest whispered to Michael.

As more people entered the church, the two continued to scale stairs upon stairs until they reached the cupola that overlooked the city of Florence. Just as Michael was beginning to enjoy the view, the lecture for the day began.

"Michael, faith is God's greatest gift to us. It is the strongest power in the world; nothing can rival it. It is the reason that Daniel survived the lion's den and not just a den of squirrels. It's the reason that David beat up on Goliath instead of some old man. Quite simply, faith can conquer all. Unfortunately, though, Michael, faith for the most part is discarded and replaced with fear. Fear that leads to sin, true sin. Do you know what true sin is in the eyes of your Creator? It is falling short. Falling short of becoming your best, making the transition from the bleachers to the field. Anyone can sit in church and talk to their God. The real work begins when you leave church and take action. Those people you saw praying when you came in, they are too busy talking to God to hear Him. Prayer and faith is about listening to God, not treating Him like Santa Claus with a list of our likes and dislikes. And when people don't hear God, they operate on fear. Instead of worrying about the message, we're too concerned with the messenger. We have countless religions not out of love, but out of fear. Religion convinces people that life is supposed to be some kind of an obstacle course. Religion is man's creation, not God's. Michael, if you truly possessed absolute faith, would it ever be necessary to talk to God on your knees?

"God made us all in his image, like eagles. But he sent Jesus down to figure out why we were acting like a bunch of chickens. Michael, you are here to realize and understand that God loves you. Where there is love, there cannot be fear. Faith is tough, it's not for the weak of heart. Faith will challenge you, wake you up, force you to grow. It is a seven-days-a-week job, which invites you to put down the paper cross you might be carrying and step out from the masses of mediocrity. Michael, God's message to you is, and always has been, inside of you. In your heart, as you learned yesterday. If you truly love God, you honor this message and don't question it. You begin to act on it. Faith, Michael, where there is faith, there can only be miracles. And where there is fear, there can only be misery.

"Besides, the true religion of the world isn't that of God's Word. It's that of other people's opinion. It dictates where we work, what we wear, and sometimes even whom we marry. It's pretty influential. Trust God. Don't allow His Word to become second in line to others. I don't think God really cares one way or the other if we go to Mass on Sunday, especially if we choose to worship at the altar of fear the other six days of the week.

"Take God's love, Michael, and go to new levels in your life. Simply put, become You. It's funny, Michael, but most people don't realize that the road to their dreams and the road to their fears are the same degree of difficulty. The reason behind which road we select is your next lesson. Remember, with faith, all things are possible."

As the Priest ended his lecture, he stared out at the mountains that surrounded the city, pleased by his own words and hopeful that Michael would apply them to his life. Michael hugged the priest and began the long trek down the stairs, then disappeared into the streets of the world's most beautiful city.

Michael returned to his apartment, opened his notebook, and began to reflect on what he had heard. He realized that God spoke to us in our hearts and that His message usually contained our treasure. Then, if we have faith, we carry out the message, but if we lack faith and operate on fear, we ignore the message. Not bad for just two days, Michael thought.

He closed his notebook. The rest of his day would be spent window-shopping. Even though his lack of funds limited his purchasing power, he simply enjoyed the atmosphere out on the streets. He passed by the leather market outside San Lorenzo and began to witness the comical arguments. All the vendors spoke fluent English, except when a tourist tried to lower the price that was being asked for one of their items. Then you'd be lucky to get a yes or a no. Either way, it was cheap entertainment and beat watching reruns of American sitcoms on the TV in his apartment.

Falling asleep used to be difficult for Michael, with everyone in the world driving a moped under his window, but for the last two nights he didn't even hear their buzzing. Michael fell asleep, dreaming of tomorrow's trip to the museum and his visit with the Curator.

CHAPTER FIVE

Wednesday morning saw Michael skip breakfast and head over to the Academia, the museum where he was to meet the Curator for his next lesson. Upon reaching the building the sign on the door said "closed", but Michael went ahead and opened it. He knew it would be open for the same reason that the doctor and the priest had been expecting him.

Michael headed down the corridor and saw no one, with the exception of a few statues that lined the walls. "Come along now, Michael," spoke a voice from nowhere. "Let's begin while we have the museum to ourselves," said the Curator, a balding man who appeared to be in his fifties. He led Michael down a hallway that brought the two to the large room that contained the lesson for that day. There it stood, Michelangelo's magnificent sculpture of the biblical hero, David. Michael had seen pictures of the statue before in textbooks, on postcards, but had been too lazy to appreciate it in person. Now, its lifelike quality surprised the American.

"Lesson three will begin with work on your part, Michael. Please, study the statue for a few minutes and tell me what it is that you see."

The Curator was looking for a message. What was the message behind the masterpiece?

After a few minutes, Michael arrived at his answer. "I see a person who has complete confidence in himself and his task," finished Michael, awaiting the Curator's response.

"That's pretty accurate Michael. Open your notebook up and take down the following..."

Wednesday-Be Your Own Hero

"Be your own hero, Michael. I dare you!

"I believe that your last discussion ended with the priest explaining how each of us chooses certain roads in life. People either walk the road of their dreams or the road of their fears. Each road is filled with the same amount of smiles and tears; however, it is the opinion that you hold of yourself that will ultimately dictate which road you select. Will you walk the road that leads up the mountain of your dreams, or will your road take you simply around the block, over and over again?

"As children, we all have our hero's posters up on our walls. We are secure in the knowledge that one day we shall take their place. We have strong images of ourselves and have no doubts about our shot at greatness. Michael, you are on the steps of adulthood, and you will soon face a decision. Will you keep the posters up on the wall, or will you take the posters off the wall and become your own hero? The decision you make is ultimately based on the opinion that you hold of yourself. Are you David? Or are you a second-class citizen?

"Look into the eyes of David. Do you see any doubt? I didn't think so. When Michelangelo began this project, he stated that his depiction of the biblical hero would be before he slayed Goliath. His look and aura is one of knowing and expectation. We all share this same strength and courage when we choose to find our treasure and follow our dreams. David doesn't doubt his ability to tackle life or his fears. Why should you, or anyone else for that matter? Maturity is calling, Michael, and you must decide where your attention and energy will follow, your dreams or your fears.

"Promise me one thing, Michael. Promise me that you shall refuse to mire in mediocrity. Trust in the image that God created, which is you. Remember, God makes miracles, not minnows."

With that statement, the Curator's words came to an end. He continued to stare at the statue of David, all the while expecting Michael to be doing the same. "Fix that image of David into your mind, Michael. Keep it there forever, and when doubt comes knocking at your door, make sure that David answers."

The Curator disappeared into the next room and Michael remained motionless. He continued to look at the statue, imprinting an image onto his mind that cannot be gotten from a postcard. He realized the statue and the parable from the Bible echoed the idea of faith, the idea on which the Priest's discussion had focused. God was the central theme behind most of the lectures that he had heard. Michael also realized that he had always prayed to God, yet, never listened to Him.

Those visitors waiting in line on the sidewalk stared at Michael as he left the museum, wondering how he had gained access before the doors opened. Michael stared at them and the cameras around their necks. He wondered if they were merely going to take endless pictures of Michelangelo's statue, or if they would actually look at it, stare into its eyes, and understand its message. Their loss, Michael thought to himself, convinced they would choose the former of the two options.

Wednesday afternoon saw Michael mail some postcards home as well as take his daily stroll throughout the town square. Each day he discovered a new store, a hidden street, or a centuries-old church. The city was always filled with activity, yet it was carried out in a relaxed manner. The Florentines took a siesta every day and always made time a priority. Michael had heard that in Italy, people work to live. In America, however, we live to work. The Florentines seemed to have mastered the art of living. They found pleasure in routine chores that Americans seemed to do with a blank stare on our face. And they also found pleasure in simply relaxing and doing nothing. Had these people found their treasures?

CHAPTER SIX

Thursday morning brought with it more sunshine and clear skies as Michael rode his bicycle out of town and into the hills of Fiesole that surrounded the city. His notebook rattled around the basket as he began searching for the farmhouse where he was to again meet a nameless, unknown person. Signore Vernola's itinerary labeled the man as simply the Farmer. Michael wondered what his fourth lesson would center on, as he eyed the farmhouse with green shutters, surrounded by tall fruit trees and bearing the proper address from the napkin.

Michael balanced his bike against a fence and knocked on the door. The door stayed shut as Michael headed around to the back of the house. There was no Farmer, or anyone for that matter, to be seen. Michael took a seat at an old wooden table and decided to simply wait.

"I'm coming, Michael, please stay seated," came a voice from somewhere. The Farmer descended a ladder propped against a nearby tree and greeted Michael. "Sorry, I was up in the tree gathering some apples. I hope you had an easy ride here."

Michael figured that the simplicity of their sur-roundings might be echoed in the lesson, so he kept his notebook closed, as the two began to chatter. The Farmer was also without an Italian accent, another one of Uncle Sam's men. Michael still was curious as to why this most Italian of journeys was without, well, any Italians.

"Michael," the Farmer began. "I think it is very important that each of us try to find God. I was never able to find Him in church, though. Sure, His image is everywhere, in the windows, the ar-chitecture, the hymns of the choir, as well as the words of the priest. But I never found God, simply His image, in a museum kind of way. Take this down, please…"

Thursday-You Can Always Find God In Nature

"Michael, I watch the birds fly and the fish swim. Each animal is aware of its particular role, and knows that it is always cared for. It will al-ways have food and shelter. Have you ever seen a fish try to fly, Michael? It's funny, though; the people who should be singers are selling insurance, and those who should be writers are glued to a desk at some bank. People are clouded with uncertainty as to their roles in the drama that is life. Michael, the next time you see a flock of birds in flight, pay special attention. A bird never focuses on falling. Its only concern is its destination, and it never doubts its ability to get there. Neither should you once you've selected your life's path.

"I also used to think that I only enjoyed three hundred and sixty-five days of sunshine each year. But you know, the sunshine's a whole lot brighter after a few days of rain. Don't frown at the rainy days of life, Michael. Enjoy them, learn from them, as they signal the rebirth and renewal that is just around the corner. The trees must lose their leaves in order to gain new ones, and life is about the same change. Change that is constant and guaranteed. To try and fight it is a waste of your time and energy. Accept change, because change is an invitation to a stronger you. Progress can be made only when you relax to the circumstances of life, not when you attempt to fight them. Besides, Michael, you are the only person whom you can control. Work on you, keep your power, don't give it away to your surroundings."

The Farmer smiled at Michael and offered him a quick snack of bread and cheese. Michael accepted, and when they were finished they said goodbye, confident that this was their first and last visit together.

Michael glided back toward town on his bicycle, allowing the slope of the hill to do most of the work. His mind drifted to the bookstore owner and how their meeting had seemed almost magical. It also came to his attention that all the teachers were awaiting his company, and all were Americans. Either way, it seemed to Michael that he had learned a great deal over the past four days. As the road leveled out, Michael began to pedal again, thinking ahead to Sunday's lesson.

Michael rode his bike down to the Arno River, where he threw his bike down and spent the rest of the afternoon watching all the crew teams rowing down the rusty-colored river. He opened up his notebook and reviewed his lessons for the week and wondered about those to come.

CHAPTER SEVEN

Friday's lesson was to take place at an elementary school on Via Cavour, where he was scheduled to meet with the Teacher. As he biked to his meeting, the noise of children alerted him that he was nearing the school. Eyeing the playground, he threw his bike in the rack that was situated in front of the school where he was immediately greeted.

"Good morning, Michael," said the Teacher without any trace of an Italian accent. The two headed through the doors of the school, to the outdoors, where the elementary school-aged kids were at play.

"Michael, pay attention to these kids; don't let their age throw you. Believe it or not, each one of these children is a genius. Do you remember when you were a child, Michael? You were all powerful, just like these kids. From your backyard, you could visit anywhere in the world, be anyone, and accomplish anything. Your future was filled with possibilities. You couldn't wait to grow up. Each passing birthday allowed you to thrust another finger in the air to show the world your gain in years. Let me guess. Those possibilities have become responsibilities, and all that "want to" is becoming "have to." What about your focus? Is it ever on today, which is the most important day of all? Instead, your mind is probably on a past that will never return or a future that has yet to occur. These kids on the slide, their biggest concern is what's for lunch.

"Do you remember waking up to the season's first snowfall? You probably had butterflies that were doing flips in your stomach, as you couldn't wait to get outside. Open your book up Michael, and take down the following…"

Friday-Don't Ever Lose The Butterflies In Your Stomach

"Always find wonder with the world, Michael; stare at the stars, jump in the puddles, and taste the snow. With the mind of a child, all things are possible. Remember that! Don't let Flintstones vitamins become Prozac, or Cinderella become Silence of the Lambs. These kids are addicted to life, not substances. They choose to believe in

Santa Claus, and what's the harm? Either way, the presents still end up under the tree and the cookies that you left out get eaten. The movies you watched as a child filled you with wonder and invited you to try the impossible. As you grow older, you lose this wonder. Then the only way movies can grab your attention is by shocking you. You are so dulled to the magic of life that news of someone's death or a plane going down grabs your attention. Do you know why? Not yet, for that is your next lesson. Remember, Michael, growing up is different than growing old. Don't ever lose those butterflies and you'll do okay."

Michael openly thanked the Teacher and then mentally thanked the kids who were still at play, oblivious to his presence.

He headed home to church bells ringing, cars battling pedestrians, and old men in conference with childhood friends.

Instead of going out, he stayed in bed the rest of the day and read. Every few minutes he put down his book to reflect on the lesson at the playground.

The Teacher was right, Michael thought. As a child, you can walk into any bookstore, open up any children's book and find that they all read the same: "You are a miracle. You can do anything you want. There has never been another Danny, Michael or David. You're one of a kind!" But, two rows down is the self-help aisle, which means we forgot those messages along the way. The Little Engine That Could must have run out of gas!

The Duomo's bells struck eleven. Michael turned his lights out and began to dream. Two days to go.

CHAPTER **EIGHT**

Saturday was an appropriate day for Michael's trip to the cemetery for Lesson Six. Clouds and rain accompanied him on his walk over the Ponte Vecchio to the other side of the Arno. He saw the graveyard at the top of the hill and began to climb the stairs to the cemetery. He wondered what he could possibly take away from this lesson.

The Gravedigger dropped his shovel to extend a handshake to Michael. He tried to welcome Michael to the ominous surroundings, if such a thing were possible.

"Hello, Michael. I apologize that we are ending your week on what appears to be a sour note. However, it is one of life's most difficult lessons to tackle and then comprehend." The rain began to fall heavier on the two, although neither seemed to notice.

"Michael, are you afraid to die? Don't answer, simply focus on it and hear me out. Because it is through facing death that we can lead a truly wonderful life." The Gravedigger's pleasant demeanor belied the locale of his employment. "If you are afraid of death, Michael, then you are afraid of God. You are going to die, Michael. It is one of the few givens in life, yet continues to be our number one fear. It is the reason that our churches are constantly packed, regardless of denomination. It is the reason people wear black to funerals, as if the deceased is truly going to rot in the ground for eternity. It is the reason that we say our Hail Marys, the reason that Jesus' image is on our dashboards, and the reason that people live life at a breakneck speed. We eat while we're driving, exercise while reading the newspaper, and raise our kids while watching TV. We rush here, go there, the entire time running from death.

"For all our religions, the fear still exists, which means it isn't being alleviated. We continue to take the eleven o'clock news to bed with us, only to wake up to a front page of horrors that have little to do with us.

"Michael, if you had only two weeks to live, where would you be? Who would you be with? What would you do? Well, since you're probably near twenty, you have about twenty-five hundred weeks left. Not a hell of a whole lot, is it? You had better begin to live your life and not someone else's.

"What about death? Well, it's no big deal. You simply lose your body, your temporary traveling suit. Then when all is said and done, you shall return home to God. Don't insult God by fearing what you believe to be the end. It isn't. This journey that everyone feels to be so,.. so permanent, is only temporary. We are here to love and to learn. Honor God by doing both. And when the time comes for someone other than myself to bury your body, remember, your body may be here, but you won't. You'll be going home. Open your book up, Michael, and write the following…"

Saturday-Understand Death.
Don't Run From It.

"Thanks, Michael."

The Gravedigger picked up his shovel and left Michael among the rows of tombstones. Michael followed the man to ask his first question of the week.

"Excuse me, sir, but why are you and the rest of my teachers all Americans?"

The Gravedigger was charmed by the question, since he had asked the same question himself some thirty years before.

"Michael, I have work to do. You have all day Sunday to reflect upon your week, and I'm sure you'll come up with the answer on your own. Goodbye and good luck to you."

Michael smiled, and behind his joy was a touch of sadness that his teachings had come to an end.

Michael passed the Ponte Vecchio. As he headed home, he thought about dropping by the bookstore to surprise Signore Vernola, but he knew the bookseller would be disappointed in Michael. Sunday's goal was in Michael's hands. Could he come up with the most important lesson of all?

CHAPTER NINE

Sunday morning came soon enough, and Michael threw on a baseball cap and headed out the door with his notebook in hand. He decided to spend his day at the Piazzale Michelangelo, where he would be afforded the opportunity for some solitude as he reflected on his lessons. When Michael arrived, he was surprised to find that he was not alone. He was sharing the view with a few young couples and starving artists who were trying to discover yet another way to render the city's skyline more impressively. The Piazzale looked out on the city of Florence in a way that allowed its entire splendor to shine. Michael gazed upon the city that now seemed a great deal like his home, even though he had spent but six months there. He reflected on all he had learned and seen. Michael thought that it was nice to finally receive a true education in living, since it is never addressed in schools or society. They tell you how to add and subtract, who led countries into war, yet never a word on how to play the game of life in a manner that lets you approach it with a smile.

A few hours passed and the streets down below began to fill up with all the worshippers leaving mass at the Duomo. Some were heading home, others were on their way to the soccer stadium for the day's match. While Catholicism was the true religion of Italy, soccer ran a very close second, even on Sundays.

Michael continued to watch the people and think about the most valuable thing that he had learned during his stay here. What lesson would he take away that was the most important? Michael relaxed and began to come to the realization that he believed Signore Vernola knew he would. In a world where we are forever surrounded by people, places, and things, Michael had the opportunity to escape and was forced to spend time with someone he had never met before, himself. Michael clicked his pen and next to Sunday wrote...

I Know Myself

This in Michael's mind was the most important thing he would take back to the States with him. He also knew that the true challenge in life is to have the courage to be oneself in a world that welcomes conformity. Michael put his pen down and smiled. He smiled at those who had taught him a great deal about life, life that is to be lived and experienced during our short time here on Earth.

Night came soon, and Michael realized that he had one last stop to make. He needed to return to the bookstore, not only to thank the bookseller for sending him on an unforgettable journey, but more importantly to inform him of his latest insight. On his way to the bookstore, he suddenly realized the answer to the question he had asked the Gravedigger. All six of his teachers were Americans because they had visited Florence some time ago, also as students, and they, too, had embarked on the weeklong trip prescribed by the old Italian. They all had the same questions Michael did when they first wandered into the old bookstore. Michael laughed to himself and wondered if they needed a Teacher for Sunday.

Michael saw the sign that read "After Dark," the name of Vernola's store. Nine o'clock was drawing near and he didn't want to keep the Italian waiting. The store was empty, which was to be expected for a Sunday night, as most people were home with their families.

CHAPTER TEN

A young woman stood behind the counter when Michael came in. She was eyeing the clock, waiting for her nightlife. Michael approached her, not daring to use his Italian.

"Excuse me Miss, is Signore Vernola in tonight?" Michael anxiously awaited her affirmative answer, since just a week ago Vernola had assured him that they would have the opportunity to exchange their farewells.

The woman stared at Michael and hesitantly responded in a thick Tuscan accent, "Vernola... he owned the store some thirty years ago. He sold it to my father and it's been in our family ever since. I'm awfully sorry, but the man you are seeking passed away a long time ago. I remember meeting him once as a little girl, though. Would you care to speak to my father? He's in the back. I'd be glad to go and get him."

Michael couldn't respond to the woman's question. All he could do was to hurriedly race out of the store, a dazed look on his face, trying to ignore the clerk's comments. He knew in his heart that the past week had not been a dream, anymore than their encounter one week earlier in the bookstore.

Michael found himself roaming the streets for a while. He didn't feel like being alone in his apartment. He came upon a small piazza where an elderly bag lady was busy feeding pigeons. She seemed perfectly content with the silence of the night, in the company of the old buildings that surrounded her. Nevertheless, Michael approached her and offered her a few lire, nothing more than an American dollar. The old woman smiled politely at Michael while nodding what would be "no thank you" in any language. Michael smiled back at her and decided to continue his walk when the old woman spoke to him.

"Young man," she said in English, as Michael wondered what she could possibly need besides some company.

"Yes?" responded Michael.

"Did you come up with the most important lesson of all?" she asked.

Hiding the chills and goosebumps that ran up and down his spine, all Michael could muster was an affirmative nod.

The woman smiled at him and said, "Bravo, Michael, Bravo."

THE END